VALLEY COMMUNITY LIBRARY
739 RIVER STREET
PECKVILLE, PA 18452
 (570) 489-1765
www.lclshome.org

In Memory of

Barry Cornell

donated by

Mr. and Mrs. Dave

Rebovich

INSIDE MEN'S COLLEGE BASKETBALL™

BASKETBALL IN THE BIG 12 CONFERENCE

rosen publishing's
rosen central®

New York

MICHAEL A. SOMMERS

To Lui and MPS

Published in 2008 by The Rosen Publishing Group, Inc.
29 East 21st Street, New York, NY 10010

Library of Congress Cataloging-in-Publication Data

Sommers, Michael A., 1966–
Basketball in the Big 12 Conference / Michael A. Sommers. — 1st ed.
    p. cm. — (Inside men's college basketball)
Includes bibliographical references and index.
ISBN-13: 978-1-4042-1384-5 (library binding)
1. Big 12 Conference—Juvenile literature. 2. Basketball—United States—Juvenile literature. 3. College sports—United States—Juvenile literature. I. Title.
GV885.49.B55 2008
796.3230973—dc22

2007032645

Manufactured in the United States of America

On the cover: Top: Kansas State players watch from the bench as Missouri shoots free throws in the final seconds of a suspenseful 2006 game, which the Missouri Tigers won 74–71. Bottom: On his way to National Player of the Year honors, University of Texas's Kevin Durant (35) dribbles past a Texas A&M defender during the teams' showdown on February 28, 2007. Texas won the game, 98–96, in double overtime.

CONTENTS

INTRODUCTION

For fast-paced excitement, athletic grace, and down-to-the-buzzer suspense, it's hard to beat college basketball. In fact, it was through college games that the sport became so popular in the United States. Although the National Basketball Association (NBA) was formed in 1949, it wasn't until the early 1970s that professional basketball really caught on. For decades, it was college ball that kept fans glued to their seats.

Year after year, the NCAA (National Collegiate Athletic Association) championship tournament games, which take place in March and April, are the most highly rated television events of the year. In addition, close to a million fans attend the games to root for their favorite teams. During these games, college players earn an enormous amount of attention as they demonstrate their

Fans watch the Texas Longhorns play their rivals, the Texas A&M Aggies, at the University of Texas's Frank C. Erwin Center.

considerable talents and their own distinctive styles and personalities. Of course, one of the motivations fueling these athletes' performances is a chance to make it to the NBA.

Among some of the most talented coaches, players, and teams of all time have been those that make up the Big 12 Conference. In existence just a little over a decade, this group of twelve teams from the Midwest and South has already left its mark on college ball and made a place for itself in basketball history.

History of Big 12 Basketball

All levels of college basketball are popular with fans. However, of the three divisions, the most eagerly watched games are played by the group of teams in what is known as Division I.

The division system was invented by the National Collegiate Athletic Association (NCAA). Created in 1906, the NCAA is a volunteer group that organizes and sets rules for most of the college athletic programs in the United States. As of the 2006–2007 season, 336 colleges and universities from forty-nine American states boast Division I basketball teams (only Alaska has none). Within the division, teams play in different groups known as conferences. There are thirty-one different conferences, formed according to U.S. geographical location, such as the Atlantic Coast Conference, the Missouri Valley Conference, and the Pacific-Ten Conference. These and a handful of others, including the Big 12, are considered by the public and the media to be "major" conferences.

The Big 12 Conference

Although many of the teams that make up the Big 12 have been in existence for close to a century, the actual Big 12 Conference has been around for only a little over a decade. The Big 12 was born on February 25, 1994, when eight Midwest college teams (originally known as the Big Eight Conference) joined together with four Texas schools that had been members of the former Southwest Conference. The twelve universities and colleges that make up the Big 12 are Baylor University, University of Colorado, Iowa State University, University of Kansas, Kansas State, University of Missouri, University of Nebraska, University of Oklahoma, Oklahoma State University, University of Texas, Texas A&M University, and Texas Tech University.

Desmond Mason (34) of the Oklahoma State Cowboys shoots against Missouri during the Big 12's first season in 1997.

The first full Big 12 basketball season began in 1996–1997. Initially, however, it took some time for fans and sportscasters to begin generating excitement about the Big 12. After all, the Big Eight Conference went back to 1907 and had a very loyal support base.

Conference Games

When the Big 12 first began, it was decided that each season, all teams would play sixteen conference games. Over the span of a season, which extends from November through March, each team plays one game (and often two) against the other eleven teams. This has made traditional Big Eight fans happy, since they are assured that longstanding rival teams will be treated to at least one major, electrically charged showdown. Over the years, such rivalries have been nurtured by players, coaches, and especially fans.

At the end of the regular season, in early March, the Big 12 teams battle it out to see who will claim the conference title at the Big 12 tournament championship game. Four rounds are played before a victor emerges. The victorious team is automatically invited to play against other top U.S. college teams in the NCAA

Hoop History

Basketball was invented on a cold December day in 1891 at a YMCA (Young Men's Christian Association) in Springfield, Massachusetts. A group of teenage boys were feeling frustrated that they couldn't go outside to play baseball or run track. The director of the physical education program dared one of his employees, a Canadian doctor and educator named James Naismith, to come up with a game that could be played indoors in a gym. Naismith hung two peach baskets from a ten-foot-high (three meters) overhang, found an old soccer ball, and invented a game with thirteen basic rules that borrowed elements from football, soccer, and hockey. His students loved the game so much that they didn't want to leave the gym. The simple yet exciting game became known as basketball.

Since basketball could be played on any surface and required little equipment, it could be played anywhere and by anybody. Playgrounds and gymnasiums across North America were soon echoing with the thunk of rebounds.

Forward Brandon Rush (25) of the Kansas Jayhawks scores against the Texas Longhorns during the finals of the 2007 Big 12 championship tournament.

championship tournament, one of the sporting world's most prestigious and popular events.

March Madness

Every year, American sports fans are overcome by a frenzy known as March Madness. "March Madness" and "the Big Dance" are nicknames given to the NCAA basketball tournament, which extends from the first week of March through the first week of April.

Each of the 336 Division I men's basketball teams dreams of making it to the tournament and becoming the national champ.

CURRENT BIG 12 TEAMS AND THEIR ACCOMPLISHMENTS

	SCHOOL	TEAM NAME	YEAR JOINED BIG 12	BIG 12 REGULAR SEASON CONFERENCE CHAMPIONSHIPS	BIG 12 TOURNAMENT TITLES	ALL-TIME NCAA TOURNAMENT APPEARANCES
NORTH DIVISION	University of Colorado	Buffaloes	1996	0	0	10
	Iowa State	Cyclones	1996	2	1	13
	University of Kansas	Jayhawks	1996	7	5	36
	Kansas State	Wildcats	1996	0	0	22
	University of Missouri	Tigers	1996	0	0	21
	University of Nebraska	Cornhuskers	1996	0	0	6
SOUTH DIVISION	Baylor University	Bears	1996	0	0	4
	University of Oklahoma	Sooners	1996	1	3	24
	Oklahoma State	Cowboys	1996	1	2	22
	University of Texas	Longhorns	1996	1	0	25
	Texas A&M	Aggies	1996	0	0	8
	Texas Tech	Red Raiders	1996	0	0	14

However, only sixty-five teams receive invitations to the "Dance." Thirty-one teams (the winners of each of the thirty-one conferences) receive an automatic invite. The other participants are chosen at the season's end by a committee that makes its decisions based on the teams' season records.

Once participants are chosen, they are divided into four regions based on their geographical location. After an opening round, in which the sixty-fifth- and sixty-fourth-ranked teams play each other, teams battle it out in regional tournaments. Over the course of three weeks—with pressure mounting each round—games are

ALL-TIME NCAA TOURNAMENT WINS/LOSSES (winning percentage)	ALL-TIME NCAA FINAL FOUR APPEARANCES	ALL-TIME NCAA CHAMPIONSHIPS	BIG 12 CONFERENCE PLAYERS OF THE YEAR	FIRST-ROUND NBA DRAFT PICKS
9–12 (.429)	2	0	0	6
12–13 (.480)	1	0	2	7
76–36 (.679)	12	2	5	19
27–26 (.509)	4	0	0	5
18–21 (.462)	0	0	0	13
0–6 (.000)	0	0	0	3
3–6 (.333)	2	0	0	3
32–24 (.571)	4	0	1	6
37–21 (.638)	6	2	1	8
29–28 (.509)	3	0	2	7
6–9 (.400)	0	0	0	3
8–15 (.348)	0	0	0	1

played until the number of teams is pared down from sixty-four to sixteen (known as the Sweet Sixteen), and then to eight finalists (the Elite Eight). The four winners to emerge victorious from each regional tournament are called the Final Four.

By the Final Four, both the suspense and stakes are sky high. Having survived the madness of March, the four remaining teams battle it out in April for the championship crown. Winning one game means a trip to the finals. Winning a second game spells victory, accompanied by the time-honored tradition of the team hanging a national championship banner from the rafters of their school's home

The banners signifying Oklahoma State's athletic success are hung from the rafters over the court of OSU's Gallagher-Iba Arena.

arena. In addition to trophies, the winning team also takes home the actual floor from the arena where the final game was played. What the school does with this unusual award varies: some schools sell pieces to fans, others put it in storage, and still others put it to use when they decide to build new arenas of their own.

Since the Big 12 came into existence, its teams have yet to bring home a national championship. However, several have made it to the Final Four, among them Kansas in 2002 and 2003, Texas in 2003, and Oklahoma State in 2004. Prior to the birth of the Big 12, Kansas (in 1988 and 1952) and Oklahoma State (in 1945 and 1946), known at the time as Oklahoma A&M, were crowned national champs.

Unforgettable Big 12 Coaches

Over the years, the Big 12 schools have had many celebrated coaches who have inspired players, thrilled fans and sports commentators, and achieved exciting victories. However, since the Big 12 Conference was inaugurated in 1996, there have been three coaches, in particular, who have left their marks on the world of college basketball.

Roy Williams

Roy Williams, who was head basketball coach for the Kansas Jayhawks from 1988 to 2003, is a man most players regarded as a friend and a father figure. Considered one of the best college basketball coaches in the country, Williams knows everything there is to know about the game. He recruited Jayhawks players, taught game plays, and made decisions under pressure like few others.

The Kansas Jayhawks' head coach, Roy Williams, shouts instructions to his team during a timeout called during the semifinal round of the 2002 NCAA men's Final Four.

Growing up in North Carolina, Williams played basketball during high school and college. After beginning his coaching career at a local high school, he returned to the college he attended, the University of North Carolina. UNC is renowned for its top-ranked Tar Heel basketball team, and Williams served as assistant to one of the great coaches of all time, Dean Smith. During his coaching years at UNC, Williams proved he had good instincts when he helped recruit a promising young player named Michael Jordan.

Then, in 1988, Williams was offered his first head-coach position, for the Kansas Jayhawks. At the time, the Jayhawks, one of the oldest and best teams in the country, had just won the 1988 NCAA championship. Although many coaches might have found that victory a hard act to follow, Williams wasn't one of them. While Kansas didn't win another national victory under Williams, it did win almost everything else. The team went down in hoop history as the winningest team of the 1990s. In seven Big 12 seasons, the Jayhawks won ninety-four games and lost only eighteen, capturing the regular season title in 1997, 1998, 2002, and 2003. They also won the Big 12 championship title in 1997, 1998, and 1999. Furthermore, in the 2001–2002 season, Kansas became the first—and so far only—team to win every one of its Big 12 season games. Although the Jayhawks missed winning the NCAA championship title, they made the tournament every year except for one (1989). In 1991, 1993, 2002, and 2003, they reached the Final Four.

While Williams helped the Jayhawks perform at the top of their game, Kansas also made Williams look good. At KU, Williams won more games at a single school than anyone else in NCAA history. During his tenure, he earned National Coach of the Year honors in 1990, 1991, 1992, and 1997. In addition, he was elected Big 12 Coach of the Year in 1997, 2002, and 2003. His crowning glory came in 2003, when he joined his mentor, Dean Smith, as a recipient of the prestigious John R. Wooden Legends of Coaching Award for lifetime coaching achievement.

Billy Gillispie

In an interview published in the *Dallas Morning News*, Billy Gillispie's mother, Wimpy Gillispie, admitted that she has no idea whether her son eats three square meals a day or gets enough sleep because the only times she ever sees him are Christmas Eve or

Texas A&M coach Billy Gillispie argues a call during a 2007 battle against Texas Tech.

when she goes to watch an Aggies basketball game. Indeed, until recently, attending a Texas A&M basketball game or practice was the only surefire way to see Billy Gillispie, the Aggies' beloved head coach. The reason for this is that ever since he was a young boy growing up in Texas, Gillispie's whole life has revolved around basketball.

Aside from his passion for the game, Gillispie proved he was a great coach in 2004, when he was hired as Texas A&M's head coach. In the words of the *New York Times'* sports columnist Pete Thamel, A&M had long been considered a "basketball coaching graveyard." However, Gillispie's excellent recruiting skills, focus on defense, and dedication to hard work led to one of the most historic turnarounds in college basketball. The season before Gillispie joined the team, the Aggies hadn't won a single Big 12 game. Furthermore, they had had only one winning season in the previous eleven years. Yet, during 2004–2005, the Aggies won their first eleven games, a feat that earned them the honor of being the nation's most improved college team. The following season, not only did the Aggies have the best conference finish and most wins since the start of the Big 12, but for the first time ever they made it to the NCAA tournament.

The best was still to come. During the 2006–2007 season, the Aggies were ranked number six in the nation, a historical first for the team. They put on a great show during the Big 12 regular season, with a second-place finish behind the Kansas Jayhawks. However, their biggest accomplishment was making it to the Sweet Sixteen during March Madness (they tragically lost by one point, 65–64, to the Memphis Tigers). However, a bigger loss for the team came after the tournament. The Aggies had been all too aware that in his twenty-year career, their coach had never stayed at one job for more than three seasons. Despite this knowledge, players and fans went into mourning when, after three seasons, Gillispie—who had just won his second Big 12 Coach of the Year Award—suddenly decided to trade his head-coaching job at A&M for the one at the University of Kentucky.

Married to His Job

Although Billy Gillispie was married once, his wife grew tired of taking second place to basketball and asked for a divorce. Said Texas A&M assistant coach Alvin Brooks, in a *New York Times* interview: "A lot of people talk about 'I'm married to my work' . . . Well, this dude is truly married to his work. The coaches and the players, we're his family."

Gillispie himself, who would rather stay up until 3:00 AM watching game videos than socializing or getting a good night's sleep, admits that his life is "unbalanced." Gillispie's breakfast might consist of peanut butter crackers and Dr. Pepper (he goes grocery shopping only once every few months), but his obsession with the sport makes him one of basketball's most beloved, respected, and all-time great coaches.

Bob Knight

Bob Knight, Texas Tech's head coach, talks with players during the first round of the 2007 Big 12 tournament.

Currently head coach at Texas Tech, Bob Knight is considered both one of the best coaches in the history of college basketball and one of the most controversial. A former professional player, Knight was hired in 1971 as a coach for the Indiana University Hoosiers. Over the next thirty years, he became a hero to players and fans in the basketball-crazy state of Indiana. Known for his discipline, creativity, and fair play, Knight—who had studied military history in college—earned the nickname "the General." On the courts, the General ruled, leading the Hoosiers to three NCAA championships and being selected four times as National Coach of the Year.

The only problem was the General's temper. Over the years, he got into trouble for angry and aggressive behavior that ranged from swearing at the press to rough handling of players and even throwing a chair across the court during a game. Due to such conduct, in September 2000, Knight was asked to resign from Indiana.

However, the game wasn't over for the controversial coach. In March 2001, Knight was invited to coach the Texas Tech Red Raiders, a team that hadn't been to an NCAA tournament since 1996. Although hopes were high that the General would set the Raiders back on track, few thought it would happen so fast. During Knight's first season, Texas Tech went from eleventh place in the Big 12 Conference to a tie for third. Not only did the team's twenty-three wins constitute their most single-season victories since 1995–1996, but the Raiders also made it into the NCAA tournament. Over the next six years, the Raiders averaged twenty-one wins per season and qualified for four more NCAA tournaments. Meanwhile, Knight himself racked up some important records and honors. He earned his 880th career win in January 2007, passing retired North Carolina coach Dean Smith to become the all-time winningest coach in men's college basketball history. In March 2007, Knight was awarded the prestigious Naismith Award for Men's Outstanding Contribution to Basketball.

3 CHAPTER

Star Players in the Big 12

Although basketball is a team sport, every team has its stars: those extra-talented athletes who dazzle fans with their moves and speed, spectacular shots, and physical grace. Often the most dedicated team players, these rising stars also stand out due to that little bit of stardust that makes them so riveting to watch. In its short history, the Big 12 has seen its share of champions. The following players in particular have left their sneaker prints on the history of college ball.

Eduardo Nájera

Eduardo Nájera was born and raised in Chihuahua, Mexico. Growing up, there were two things he was sure of: that he loved shooting hoops and that he wanted to play college basketball in the United States. During high school, Nájera, an excellent rebounder, was a star on the Mexican junior national basketball team. But when he graduated in 1994, two obstacles stood in the way of his dream: no U.S. colleges had ever heard of him and he could hardly speak English.

Nájera's solution was to attend the Cornerstone Christian Academy, just across the border in San Antonio, Texas. After two years, Nájera not only had English down pat, but college coaches throughout the United States were interested in him. In 1997, he was offered a spot with the University of Oklahoma Sooners. Nájera became the team's leading scorer and rebounder and its emotional core. Moreover, by guiding the Sooners to the NCAA tournament during all four seasons he attended Oklahoma, he became one of the Sooners' all-time biggest stars.

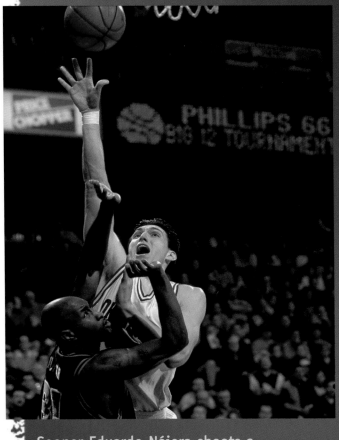

Sooner Eduardo Nájera shoots a layup during a 2000 Big 12 tournament game against the Missouri Tigers.

When Nájera graduated in 2000, he had finished in the school's all-time top ten in nine different categories and had racked up more rebounds than any other player in the Big 12 Conference for that year. He also received the Chip Hilton Player of the Year Award from the Basketball Hall of Fame, given to players who demonstrate strong personal character both on and off the court.

Popular with fans because he plays with lots of heart and fights for the rebound against much bigger players, Nájera thrilled the sports world when he was recruited by the Houston Rockets in the 2000 NBA draft. After stints playing for the Dallas Mavericks and the Golden State Warriors, he was traded to the Denver Nuggets in 2005. One of only three Mexican-born players ever to join the NBA, this 6-foot, 8-inch (2.03 meter) forward is wildly popular with Mexican and Mexican American fans. Never having forgotten his heritage, in 2004, he established the Eduardo Nájera Foundation for Latino Achievement, which provides scholarships for talented Latino students who face obstacles to their educations.

T. J. Ford

Shortly after leaving the University of Texas for a career in the pros, one of the school's most famous point guards of all time, T. J. Ford, was back with his former Longhorn teammates. It was halftime, but Ford was center court to receive an honor never before awarded in the history of Texas basketball. As the crowd chanted "T. J.!" and tears trickled down his cheeks, the 6-foot (1.83 m) basketball player received his white #11 Texas jersey from the university's athletics director. Having a jersey retired is an honor shared by only three other athletes in all of Longhorn history, and Ford definitely earned it during the two unforgettable seasons he played for Texas.

Terrance Jerod "T. J." Ford was born in Houston, Texas. By the time he reached high school, he had proved himself to be a basketball star. Dreaming of college and professional basketball careers, his ambitions seemed threatened when he was diagnosed with spinal stenosis, a medical condition in which a narrowing spinal canal pinches the spinal cord and nerves. Although this painful condition is not unusual for elderly people, it is uncommon in teenagers. However, deciding that he didn't have time for the pain, in 2001, Ford accepted an offer to play basketball for the Texas Longhorns.

During his two seasons at Texas, the point guard nicknamed the "Little Engine" certainly left his mark. Ford became the first freshman in NCAA history to lead the nation in assists, and he led his team to the NCAA tournament. In his second season, he outdid himself, leading Texas to its first Final Four since 1947. At the season's end, he received the distinguished 2003 Naismith College Player of the Year Award and the equally prestigious John R. Wooden Award.

Having been picked eighth in the first round of the 2003 NBA draft, Ford left Texas to begin his pro career playing for the Milwaukee

Texas star T. J. Ford (11) drives toward the net against the Oregon Ducks during the 2002 NCAA basketball tournament.

Bucks. A brilliant start was put on hold when Ford suffered a serious and painful spinal injury. Once again, however, Ford wouldn't let his condition get the better of him. After returning to his hometown for months of intensive physical therapy, a fully recovered Ford returned to the Bucks. He was traded in 2006 to the Toronto Raptors, where he showed fans that he hadn't lost either his intensity or his speed. As proof of the latter, in a 2007 *Sports Illustrated* survey, he was voted the fastest player in the NBA.

Showing his tremendous arm span, Longhorn superstar Kevin Durant goes on the defensive during a 2006 game against Alcorn State.

Kevin Durant

Although he turned eighteen in September 2006, Kevin Durant still had the boyish face and innocence of a fourteen-year-old. Of course, not many fourteen-year-olds are 6-feet, 9-inches (2.1 m) tall and almost universally considered the best freshman basketball player in the nation.

Lots of hard work and dedication, coupled with a winning combination of skill, athleticism, and height, allow Durant to play any offensive or defensive position. After years of dazzling crowds—and college scouts—on successful high school and American Athletic Union (AAU) teams, Durant joined the Longhorns in 2006. Said Texas coach Rick Barnes in a 2007 *Sports Illustrated* interview: "I told him when we recruited him: 'Look at Tiger Woods, Michael Jordan, the great ones . . . You're one of those guys.'"

So far, Barnes seems to be correct about his famous freshman. In one short but historic season, "K-Smoove" had a major impact on both those who play and those who watch basketball. Indeed, it's hard to ignore Durant's remarkable arm span of 7-feet, 6-inches (2.32 m) and his effortless shots and great defensive moves, not to mention his season average of 25.1 points and 11.4 rebounds per game. Such winning stats made him the Big 12 leader in scoring and rebounding, as well as the only player to make the nation's top five in both categories. Moreover, they led him to sweep the top six national player of the year honors, including the John R. Wooden Award, the Naismith Award, and the Associated Press College Player of the Year Award (in all cases, he was the first freshman in history to win). As crowning glory, during the 2007 NBA draft, Durant was selected number two overall by the Seattle Supersonics.

Acie Law IV

The day before Kevin Durant won the Wooden Award, he was on a basketball court, playing one-on-one with his friend and rival Acie Law IV of Texas A&M. If you think that Durant swept the floor with Law IV, though, think again. "He beat me three times," Durant said in an interview in the *New York Times*. "He's a great guy—he's going to have a great career."

Big 12 Award Winners

The following is a list of athletes and coaches who have won national awards in the Big 12 Conference. While there are many other awards given away each year, the ones mentioned here are a few of the most prestigious.

Naismith Men's College Player of the Year Award (awarded since 1969)
Kevin Durant, Texas, 2007
T. J. Ford, Texas, 2003

Adolph F. Rupp Trophy (College Player of the Year Award, awarded since 1972)
Kevin Durant, Texas, 2007

John R. Wooden Player of the Year (awarded since 1976)
Kevin Durant, Texas, 2007
T. J. Ford, Texas, 2003

Oscar Robertson Trophy (College Player of the Year Award, awarded since 1959)
Kevin Durant, Texas, 2007

Chip Hilton Player of the Year Award (for Personal Character On and Off the Court, awarded since 1997)
Acie Law IV, Texas A&M, 2007
Ronald Ross, Texas Tech, 2005
Eduardo Nájera, Oklahoma, 2000

John R. Wooden Legends of Coaching Award (awarded since 1999)
Roy Williams, Kansas, 2003

Naismith Men's College Coach of the Year Award (awarded since 1987)
Roy Williams, Kansas, 1997

Acie Law IV's amazing 2006 game-winning three-pointer, shot at the buzzer, quickly became known as "the Shot." Rivals.com, the Yahoo! sports site, has named it one of the top three-pointers in college basketball history.

Acie Law IV is a little bit older than his famous friend—and at 6 feet, 3 inches (1.92 m), a little bit shorter as well. The son of a college basketball player, Law grew up shooting hoops in Dallas. During high school, he attracted recruiters from several major colleges. However, because he wanted to stay at home, he chose to attend Texas A&M, enrolling in the fall of 2003. Playing point guard, Law immediately impressed teammates and fans during his freshman season with the Aggies. Early on, he earned the nickname "Captain Clutch" for his talent to take over late in the game.

"The Shot"

By the time Acie Law IV began high school, he already seemed destined for success . . . until he broke his right hand—not just once, but on three different occasions. Instead of abandoning the ball, Law's father forced him to dribble and shoot with his uninjured hand. Over time, he became just as good with his left hand as with his right.

The injuries to his right hand resulted in Law's famously accurate lefty knuckleball shot. In 2006, in a tight game that saw the Aggies battling the Longhorns for a trip to the NCAA tournament, one such shot—a buzzer-beating, game-winning three-pointer—made Aggies fans so happy that they rushed the floor. A&M fans and players still refer to Law's magic knuckleball basket as "the Shot."

Nonetheless, despite Law's efforts, the Aggies were playing poorly until 2004–2005, when legendary coach Billy Gillispie began to reverse the team's dismal fortunes. At first, many of the players, including Law, rebelled against Gillispie's tough training tactics, known as "Boot Camp." But under his guidance, the Aggies began to show their stuff. By the following season, Law was ranked among the top ten players in the Big 12 in terms of scoring, assists, and steals. Meanwhile, the Aggies made it to the NCAA tournament for the first time since 1987.

In his four years at A&M, Law established himself as one of the nation's premier point guards, a fact that led to his being taken eleventh overall in the 2007 NBA draft, by the Atlanta Hawks.

CHAPTER 4

Major Big 12 Rivalries

College basketball fans live for March Madness, when for one intense month, they watch and scream with joy or tear their hair out as sixty-five teams compete for a championship title. Regular-season games can be just as thrilling, however, due to the intense rivalries that exist between certain colleges. In college basketball, these rivalries are fought both on and off the court, and players and fans look forward to some of the showdowns for months in advance. In fact, they have become so popular that recently ESPN launched "Rivalry Week," a week during which the cable sports station broadcasts the top matchups in college basketball.

Aside from exercising time-honored traditions such as waving signs, yelling cheers and songs, and painting their faces and bodies, fans also sit back and appreciate a level of play that is often better than what March Madness has to offer. Because rivalry games tend to bring out the best in both teams, the games themselves are

At Texas A&M's Reed Arena, fans hold up copies of the student newspaper, the *Battalion*, as they cheer on the Aggies during a 2007 game against their longtime rivals, the Texas Longhorns.

often exciting and unpredictable. In the Big 12, three rivalries are of an especially fiery nature: Kansas vs. Missouri, Texas vs. Texas A&M, and Oklahoma vs. Oklahoma State.

Kansas vs. Missouri

The age-old rivalry that pits the Kansas Jayhawks against the Missouri Tigers is considered by most basketball experts to be one of the fiercest competitions in the NCAA. That the two neighboring Midwest states have long been political and economic rivals only adds to the hostility in the basketball arena. As Kansas forward

While Kansas fans try to distract him, J. T. Tiller (4) of the Missouri Tigers shoots a free throw during a 2007 game against the Kansas Jayhawks.

Nick Collison said in an interview with MSNBC: "We always want to beat Missouri. We hate them and they hate us." The teams' fierce rivalry is known as the Border War or the Border Showdown. (The name has its roots in the actual "border wars" between Kansas and Missouri, which led to the outbreak of the American Civil War, in 1861.)

Kansas has tradition on its side—after all, basketball's inventor, Dr. James Naismith, was one of the Jayhawks' first coaches. Missouri is the classic underdog, however, known to come out of nowhere and turn the tables on Kansas. To date, Kansas holds the upper hand with 163 wins against Missouri's 93, including 11 of their last 14 matchups.

Oklahoma vs. Oklahoma State

Among the most eagerly awaited rivalry games featured on ESPN's "Rivalry Week" is the matchup between the Oklahoma Sooners and the Oklahoma State Cowboys. The tension dates way back to when the schools often butted heads as two of the Big Eight Conference's leading teams. Since then, their rivalry has been known as the Bedlam Series.

Although Oklahoma boasts more wins, with 121 to Oklahoma State's 87, over the last few years the Cowboys have made a comeback. As a result, the suspense has intensified with some last-minute upsets and surprise victories.

Texas vs. Texas A&M

Texas is famous for being a football state, but if you've ever caught one of the frenzied hoop games played between the Texas Longhorns and the Texas A&M Aggies, you might start to wonder. The Lone Star Showdown that pits the University of Texas against Texas A&M brings much of Texas to a halt. When the teams meet up, as they have been doing for decades, sparks fly.

And the sparks have been brighter than ever in the last few years as both teams have ranked high in the Big 12 and in the nation. In fact, in February 2007, the matchup between the two rivals was considered one of the most exciting college basketball games ever played. In large part, this was due to the presence of celebrated Longhorn superstar Kevin Durant and Aggie phenom Acie Law IV. The two opponents—who happen to be good pals—went head-to-head in a game that went into double overtime. The Longhorns blew an eleven-point lead in the second half and trailed by seven points after the Aggies com-

Acie Law IV (1) shoots over Kevin Durant (35) during the 2007 double-overtime thriller between the Aggies and the Longhorns.

pleted a 23–5 run. Then, with ten minutes on the clock, Texas recovered, and in an excruciatingly close fashion, beat the Aggies, 98–96. As Texas coach Rick Barnes said in an article published by the Associated Press: "I'm not sure there's ever been a bigger basketball game."

Much-Loved Big 12 Mascots

College basketball wouldn't be complete without the presence of mascots. Mascots rally and entertain the fans. Every Big 12 team has its own beloved mascots, many of which have been around for decades. While some mascots are real animals, others are humans who dress up as animals. Still others are figures that represent the historic traditions of a given school or state.

Real Animals

Many sports teams are named after animals known for traits such as speed, force, and courage. Logically, the animals that inspire a team's name also become the team mascots. To the delight of fans, several of the Big 12 universities feature mascots that are actual breathing, kicking, snorting creatures.

Reveille, the "first lady of Aggieland" makes an appearance at a 2006 game against the Baylor Bears.

For example, Texas A&M has Reveille, a collie popularly known as A&M's "first lady." The original Reveille was a stray that some students snuck into their residence. The next day she gave herself away when she barked during the morning reveille (French for "wake-up call"). While it was against the rules to keep animals in the dorms, the students fell in love with the dog, and she became the Aggies' mascot. Reveille attends all of A&M's home games.

Texas Longhorn mascot Hook 'Em leads the cheering at a 2007 game against Oklahoma State.

Another popular mascot belongs to the Baylor Bears, who have a real live bear as their mascot. The bear's name is Judge, in honor of Judge Robert Emmett Bledsoe Baylor, who gave his name to the Texas university. The first of many Judges was donated in 1917 by Herbert E. Mayr, a Waco businessman who won the bear in a poker game. Currently, there are two North American black bears on campus: Judge Joy Reynolds and Judge Sue Sloan (their nicknames are Joy and Lady).

Texas Longhorn fans are proud of their mascot, a longhorn steer named Bevo. The first Bevo was purchased in 1916 to replace the previous mascot, a bulldog named Pig. When Bevo died in 1920, students grieved. Then in true Texan style, they barbecued the steer!

Let's Make a Deal

Over the years, many bears have served as Baylor mascots. One of the first and best-known came to Baylor in the 1930s. A student named Bill Boyd purchased the bear from a Waco zoo that had gone broke. Boyd then made a deal with Baylor's president at the time, Pat Neff: he would take care of the mascot in return for free tuition. Neff accepted the deal, and that was the beginning of the live-in bear mascot tradition at Baylor.

Bevo's long horns inspired the hand symbol and chant "Hook 'Em Horns," which can be seen and heard at all Texas games. When Bevo can't attend games, his costumed alter ego, named Hook 'Em, leads the cheers.

Similar in size to Bevo is the Colorado's buffalo mascot, Ralphie. The first Ralphie goes back to 1934, when a group of students rented a buffalo calf—and his cowboy keeper—for $25. However, because Ralphie's hoofs would mark up the court, the Buffs' costumed buffalo mascot, Chip, attends all basketball games.

Costumed Animals

It's not always possible—let alone safe or practical—to have a live animal as a mascot. For example, Kansas State's original mascot was a real, roaring bobcat. Keeping a wild beast in a cage didn't give fans or animal lovers much to cheer about, however. Consequently, in 1947, along came Willie Wildcat, a student who dresses up in a brown wildcat costume. Similarly, the University of Oklahoma's traditional mascot, a wagon (known as the Sooner Schooner) pulled by two white ponies, is too big to bring onto a basketball court. Therefore, Boomer and Sooner, two humans dressed as white ponies, lead their fans' cheers.

The University of Missouri's costumed mascot is a tiger named Truman. He honors a historic group of brave Missouri citizens. In the 1860s, bandits often raided small Missouri towns, causing citizens to create companies of home guards to protect themselves. One such company, called the Missouri Tigers, gained a reputation for exceptional courage. Missouri's sporting teams therefore became known as "Tigers." The name "Truman" was chosen in honor of Missouri-bred president Harry S. Truman.

From left to right, Kansas players Julian Wright, Mario Chalmers, Brandon Rush, and Micah Downs proudly hold up the Jayhawks' Baby Jay mascot during media day in October 2005.

The Kansas Jayhawk is another mascot with historic origins. In the late 1850s, a regiment of Kansas soldiers began calling themselves "Jayhawkers," inspired by a mythical bird that was a cross between a blue jay and a sparrow hawk. The term came to be associated with brave Kansans fighting for an independent state. When in 1861, Kansas was admitted to the United States as a free state, all Kansans became known as Jayhawkers. Later on, the Jayhawk became KU's symbol. The school's mascots are known as Big Jay and Baby Jay.

Animal costumes are fairly straightforward to design, but what happens if your team is named after a whirling tunnel of wind? In the early 1950s, Harry Burrell, the sports director for Iowa State's

Cyclones, came up with several costume designs but never succeeded in creating something fans would recognize as a cyclone. Eventually a student contest was held to come up with a more practical mascot. The winning idea was a cardinal, based on the school's colors of cardinal and gold. Cy seemed the obvious choice for their new mascot's name.

Traditional Figures

Most of the Big 12 schools boast regional traditions and heritages that date back decades. Reflecting this history, some Big 12 teams' mascots pay homage to traditional figures or person-

Herbie Husker entertains Nebraska Cornhuskers fans during a break in a game's action.

alities that have long been local sources of inspiration.

The Nebraska Cornhuskers, for example, have had Herbie Husker as their mascot since the 1970s. Originally, Herbie dressed in a husker's traditional outfit of jeans, boots, and a cowboy hat. In 2003, the university decided that Herbie needed a more modern look. His makeover included a new shirt and boots, and a slimmer, more toned body. While Herbie was away getting "made over," an inflatable 8-foot (2.44 m) doll named Lil' Red filled in for him. Today, both mascots are equally popular on the courts.

Each year, ten to fifteen Oklahoma State students audition for the chance to spend a year as mascot Pistol Pete, shown above.

Two other legendary figures from the Wild West are Oklahoma State's Pistol Pete and Texas Tech's Raider Red. Pete has been the Cowboys' mascot since 1923. Each year, two students share the role of playing the classic cowboy. Raider Red is also a gun-toting cowboy. The identity of the student who dresses up as the mascot is kept secret. In March 2007, fans were surprised to learn that, for the first time, a male and a female student had taken turns "playing" Red throughout the season.

Looking Ahead

As time passes, college basketball's appeal only seems to grow. Indeed, over the last few years, basketball has become even more popular. How could it not? Few other sports are so intensely filled with nonstop action, requiring players to think fast and move even faster. It is no wonder that March Madness is beginning to rival the Super Bowl as the biggest televised and online sports event. In fact, some sports observers say it's already bigger. Meanwhile, basketball is now the number-two sport in the world after soccer. No matter where they live, more people than ever are playing and watching the game that all started with an old soccer ball and two peach baskets.

assist The last pass to a teammate that leads directly to a field goal (basket).

buzzer beater A shot that's made just before the buzzer sounds to signal the end of a period.

center A player who is generally in the center of the offense, usually the tallest player on a team.

charisma Great personal magnetism or charm.

controversial Provoking debate, argument, or difference of opinion.

draft A system that professional league teams use to select new players from a choice group of amateur players. The result is that each pro team receives some of the most promising players.

dribble To bounce the ball repeatedly with one hand, while moving or standing still.

forward One of two players who usually operates near a corner, on both offense and defense, and who is often a team's highest scorer.

guards The two, usually smallest, players on each team who handle setting up plays and passing to teammates closer to the basket.

hoop The rim or basket.

mythical Imaginary, fictitious.

point guard Player who usually brings the ball up-court for his team and runs offense.

prestigious Honored, distinguished.

rebounder A player who excels at gaining possession of the basketball after it has come off the backboard.

recruit To try to acquire an athlete for a specific team.

scout A person sent out by a team to observe and recommend new talent for recruitment.

FOR MORE INFORMATION

Big 12 Conference
400 East John Carpenter Freeway
Irving, TX 75062
(469) 524-1000
Web site: http://www.big12sports.com
The Big 12 Conference consists of twelve universities and sponsors
   twenty-one different sports.

Naismith Memorial Basketball Hall of Fame
1000 West Columbus Avenue
Springfield, MA 01105
(877) 4HOOPLA (446-6752) or (413) 781-6500
Web site: http://www.hoophall.com
The Hall of Fame honors the most important figures and greatest
   players in basketball's history.

National Collegiate Athletic Association (NCAA)
700 W. Washington Street
P.O. Box 6222
Indianapolis, IN 46206-6222
(317) 917-6222
Web site: http://www.ncaa.org/wps/portal
The NCAA regulates most U.S. college and university athletic programs.

Web Sites

Due to the changing nature of Internet links, Rosen Publishing has
developed an online list of Web sites related to the subject of this book.
This site is updated regularly. Please use this link to access the list:

http://www.rosenlinks.com/imcb/bbtw

Conner, Floyd. *Basketball's Most Wanted: The Top 10 Book of Hoops' Outrageous Dunkers, Incredible Buzzer-Beaters, and Other Oddities*. Dulles, VA: Potomac Books, 2001.

Decock, Luke. *Great Teams in College Basketball History* (Great Teams). Chicago, IL: Raintree, 2006.

Einhorn, Eddie. *How March Became Madness: How the NCAA Tournament Became the Greatest Sporting Event in America*. New York, NY: Triumph Books, 2006.

Fulks, Matt. *CBS Sports Presents: Stories from the Final Four*. Lenexa, KS: Addax, 2002.

Isenhour, Jack. *Same Knight, Different Channel: Basketball Legend Bob Knight at West Point and Today*. Dulles, VA: Potomac Books, 2001.

Kerkhoff, Blair. *Greatest Book of College Basketball*. Lenexa, KS: Addax, 2002.

NCAA. *NCAA March Madness: Cinderellas, Superstars, and Champions from the NCAA Men's Final Four*. New York, NY: Triumph Books, 2004.

"Acie Law." Aggies Official Web Site of Texas A&M Athletics. Retrieved June 2007 (http://www.aggieathletics.com/bios.php?YOS=2005&PID=7270&SID=MBB).

Associated Press. "Durant Captures Wooden Award in Runaway." *New York Times*, April 8, 2007. Retrieved June 2007 (http://www.nytimes.com/aponline/sports/AP-BKC-Wooden-Award.html).

Associated Press. "Gillispie Leaves Questions for Texas A&M." *New York Times,* April 8, 2007. Retrieved June 2007 (http://www.nytimes.com/2007/04/08/sports/ncaabasketball/08aggies.html).

"Blog Q&A With . . . Texas A&M's Acie Law IV." *Sports Illustrated*, February 20, 2007. Retrieved June 2007 (http://sportsillustrated.cnn.com/si_blogs/basketball/ncaa/2007/02/blog-q-with-texas-acie-law-iv.html).

"Bob Knight: Red Raider Head Coach." Texas Tech Athletics Web Site. Retrieved June 2007 (http://texastech.cstv.com/sports/m-baskbl/mtt/knight_bob00.html).

Chad, Norman. "Couch Slouch." *Houston Chronicle*, November 20, 2006. Retrieved June 2007 (http://www.chron.com/disp/story.mpl/sports/chad/4350211.html).

Chartrand, Kristi. "Nothing Like It." CollegeHoopsNet.com. Retrieved June 2007 (http://www.collegehoopsnet.com/specials/021404.htm).

Cohen, Rachel. "Gillispie Turned Moribund A&M Around." *Dallas Morning News*, March 16, 2006. Retrieved June 2007 (http://www.dallasnews.com/sharedcontent/dws/spt/colleges/national/

tournament/ncaamen/stories/031606dnspotamulede.
1720393e.html).

"College Basketball's Best Rivalries." NBCSports.com. Retrieved June 2007 (http://www.msnbc.msn.com/id/6786719).

Garcia, Marlen. "Law Makes Turnaround, Helps Gillispie Guide Texas A&M to New Heights." *USA Today*, February 21, 2007. Retrieved June 2007 (http://www.usatoday.com/sports/college/mensbasketball/big12/2007-02-20-aggies-cover_x.htm?csp=34).

Glier, Ray, and Thayer Evans. "Gillispie Says He Is Ready for Kentucky's Expectations." *New York Times*, April 7, 2007. Retrieved June 2007 (http://www.nytimes.com/2007/04/07/sports/ncaabasketball/07kentucky.html?ref=ncaabasketball&pagewanted=print).

"History of Basketball." BetterBasketball.com. Retrieved June 2007 (http://www.betterbasketball.com/history-of-basketball).

Jackson, Scoop. "Law & Order." ESPN.com. Retrieved June 2007 (http://sports.espn.go.com/espn/page2/story?page=jackson/070312&sportCat=ncb).

"Kevin Durant." TexasSports.com. Retrieved June 2007 (http://www.texassports.com/index.php?s=&url_channel_id=16&change_well_id=17&member_id=974).

Langley, Jay. "Knight to Receive Naismith Award." *Daily Toreador*, March 30, 2007. Retrieved June 2007 (http://media.www.dailytoreador.com/media/storage/paper870/news/2007/03/30/Sports/Knight.To.Receive.Naismith.Award-2813903.shtml?reffeature=htmlemailedition).

Thamel, Pete. "Coach's 'Unhealthy' Obsession Has Led to Success at Texas A&M." *New York Times*, March 22, 2007. Retrieved June 2007 (http://select.nytimes.com/search/restricted/article?res=F60715FA3F540C718EDDAA0894DF404482).

Thamel, Pete. "Going to the Chapel?" *New York Times*, March 21, 2007. Retrieved June 2007 (http://bracket.blogs.nytimes.com/author/pthamel/2007/03/21).

"Tournament Spotlight: Eduardo Nájera." *Sports Illustrated*. Retrieved June 2007 (http://sportsillustrated.cnn.com/basketball/college/1999/ncaa_tourney/men/spotlight/news/1999/03/18/spotlight_najera).

Townsend, Brad. "A&M: Gillispie's Last College Station?" *Dallas Morning News*, February 11, 2007. Retrieved June 2007 (http://www.dallasnews.com/sharedcontent/dws/spt/colleges/texasam/stories/021107dnspoagcoach.189240a.html).

Trigg, Samuel. "Texas and Texas A&M Rivalry." Oddsboard.com. March 1, 2007. Retrieved June 2007 (http://www.oddsboard.com/article.asp?AID=101).

Wahl, Grant, and Luke Winn. "Phenomenal Freshman." *Sports Illustrated*, February 13, 2007. Retrieved June 2007 (http://sportsillustrated.cnn.com/2007/writers/grant_wahl/02/12/freshman0219).

About the Author

Michael A. Sommers was born in Texas and raised in Canada. After earning a bachelor's degree in English literature at McGill University in Montreal, Canada, he went on to complete a master's degree in history and civilizations from the École des Hautes Études en Sciences Sociales in Paris, France. For the last fifteen years, he has worked as a writer and photographer. Among the sports titles he has written for Rosen Publishing are *Snowmobiling*, *Olympic Ice Skating*, and *Football in the Big 12*.

Photo Credits

Cover (top), pp. 16, 38 © AP Photos; cover (bottom), pp. 4–5, 24, 36 (top) © University of Texas Photography Department; pp. 1, 6, 10–11, 13, 20, 29, 34 © www.istockphoto.com; p. 3 (left) © www.istockphoto.com/Benjamin Goode; pp. 7, 12, 40 © Oklahoma State University; pp. 8, 17, 27, 28, 32, 36 (bottom) © www.istockphoto.com/Bill Grove; pp. 9, 14, 18, 21, 23, 31, 39 © Getty Images; pp. 26, 30, 33, 35 © Texas A&M University.

Designer: Tom Forget
Photo Researcher: Marty Levick